"Jay Earley has taken on a v
explicating, with clear guid̶e̶....... ... ., ...
and techniques of IFS that I developed and teach but have yet
to write at length about. In this booklet, he focuses on ways to
improve the relationship between a client's Self and protective
parts and to help those parts trust Self to lead in the outside
world. Trained IFS therapists will likely find that they already
do some of what he outlines but that it is useful to have it laid
out in writing. They will also be inspired to try some new
things."

— Richard Schwartz, PhD, creator of the IFS Model,
author of *Internal Family Systems Therapy* and
You are the One You've Been Waiting For

"Challenging life situations present themselves before the client's
system is fully unburdened, and habitual protective reactions
typically take over, with the usual disastrous results. This latest
addition to Earley's professional series offers techniques for the
IFS therapist to help clients navigate this terrain. The techniques
for negotiating with protector parts, illustrated with transcripts
of sessions, include updating parts' fears, working with realistic
fears, and discerning the reasonableness of negotiating for Self-
leadership in these situations."

— Susan McConnell, Senior Lead Trainer
for the Center for Self Leadership

Books and Booklets
by Jay Earley, PhD

The IFS Series
Self-Therapy
Self-Therapy for Your Inner Critic (with Bonnie Weiss)
Resolving Inner Conflict

The IFS Professional Booklet Series
Working with Anger in IFS
Negotiating for Self-Leadership

The Pattern System^{SM} Series
Embracing Intimacy
Taking Action: Working Through Procrastination
and Achieving Your Goals
A Pleaser No Longer
Beyond Caretaking**

The Inner Critic Series (with Bonnie Weiss)
Self-Therapy for Your Inner Critic
Activating Your Inner Champion
Instead of Your Inner Critic
Letting Go of Perfectionism

Other Books
Interactive Group Therapy
Transforming Human Culture
Inner Journeys

**Forthcoming

Negotiating
for Self-Leadership

in Internal Family
Systems Therapy

Jay Earley, PhD

 **PATTERN SYSTEM BOOKS**
Larkspur, CA

Negotiating for Self-Leadership
in Internal Family Systems Therapy

▨ PATTERN SYSTEM BOOKS

140 Marina Vista Ave.
Larkspur, CA 94939
415-924-5256
www.patternsystembooks.com

Paperback ISBN-13: 978-0-9855937-1-1
LCCN: 2012947697

Printed in the United States of America

Contents

Acknowledgments

I am very grateful to Richard Schwartz, PhD, for creating the profound IFS Model, which has completely transformed not only the way I do therapy but also my teaching and writing. Susan McConnell provided wise feedback that helped me to improve this booklet.

Jeannene Langford continued her excellent work with my book covers, and Kira Freed continued her fine work of editing and proofreading.

Introduction to the
IFS Professional Booklet Series

This is one of a series of booklets that cover advanced topics in IFS theory and practice. Some of the booklets describe concepts that are well known in the professional IFS community but that haven't been put into written form before. Other booklets introduce original ideas about how to practice IFS more effectively or understand its theory in a fuller way.

In my opinion, IFS is by far the most effective and respectful psychotherapy model. At this point, it is taught mostly through an excellent professional training program rather than through writings. Therefore, the professional literature on IFS hasn't yet done justice to the profound nature of the approach. This series, along with my other IFS books, attempts to remedy this situation.

With the advent of ebooks, there is no longer a need to dispense information in the standard book length. It is now very easy to make a piece of writing any length that is appropriate. Each of these booklets will be shorter than book length yet long enough to provide you with substantial information on one specific IFS issue.

Introduction

This booklet is intended primarily for Internal Family Systems Therapy (IFS) therapists and practitioners. It assumes knowledge of the IFS view of the psyche and the IFS method. It should also be useful to therapists not trained in IFS or who are new to the IFS Model, so I have included a glossary in which the basic IFS concepts are defined.

Imagine a situation in which a client of yours has a difficult situation coming up in the next week that she asks for help with. She usually acts in a self-destructive manner in this situation, and she wants to change that. You begin to work with the protector that causes her self-destructive behavior. Once she has connected with this protector, you would ideally like to unburden the exile it is protecting so you can help this protector to relax and allow the client to interact more safely. However, she is a new client with a fair amount of trauma, so you haven't even begun to gain access to her exiles yet, and you certainly aren't going to get there today. What do you do to help her with this situation this week?

This booklet introduces a method that I call "negotiating for Self-leadership," which could benefit such a client now without waiting until you can help her exiles heal.

Internal Family Systems Therapy (IFS) is a cutting-edge psychotherapy approach that has been spreading rapidly around the country and the world over the last decade. It is the signature work of pioneering psychologist Richard Schwartz. IFS is extremely powerful for accessing deep psychological wounds and healing them. It is especially effective with trauma, and there has been increasing interest in IFS among trauma specialists. IFS is also quite effective at helping clients with everyday life issues as well as with spiritual development.

Schwartz, originally a family systems therapist, started working with his clients' inner worlds and discovered their subpersonalities, which he calls *parts*. He realized that his clients' parts were related to each other in systems that were similar to those he recognized in families, hence the name "Internal Family Systems Therapy."[1] IFS is user friendly. It is easy for clients to understand its concepts and natural for most of them to access and relate to their parts.

In following the normal IFS procedure, once you have gotten to know a protector and developed a trusting relationship with it, you ask permission to work with the exile or exiles it is protecting. The principle is that most protectors can't fully let go of their roles until the exiles they are protecting have been unburdened. Once you have permission, you go through a series of healing steps with the exile, and then you return to the protector to see if it now can let go of its protective role.

However, there are situations in which it may take quite a bit of time to heal the exiles, especially when there is trauma. It could take months to get through all the protectors

---

1. For more information on IFS, read *The Internal Family Systems Model* by Richard Schwartz, Guilford Press, 1995, and visit www.selfleadership. org.

and fully heal a traumatized exile. And if more than one exile is being protected, it may take even longer. If clients have important situations that involve a protector coming up in their lives in the next week or two, it can be very helpful to find a way to get that protector to relax before all its exiles have been healed. This calls for negotiating for Self-leadership.

There is also another situation in which negotiating for Self-leadership can be helpful. Let's say that as a result of unburdening the exiles behind a protector, it has relaxed to some extent, but it hasn't let go completely. By negotiating for Self-leadership, you can convince it to relax even more or even completely let go.

This booklet describes how to help a client to negotiate with a protector to allow the client (in Self) to handle a certain imminent life situation rather than having the protector blend with the client (as usual) and handle the situation in its extreme or dysfunctional way.

The method described in this book has been taught by Richard Schwartz in his trainings but has not been put into writing before this booklet. It includes the IFS process of *updating*, in which the client helps a protector to see that the client is a competent adult, not a vulnerable child. Updating is explained in Chapter 1.

Usually, the client will be negotiating with the protector about a situation in which the protector's fears are unrealistic because they come from childhood. Chapter 2 describes how to handle this situation. Sometimes, however, the protector's fears may have some validity in the present situation, which makes the negotiation more complicated. Chapter 3 explains how to handle this.

Chapter 4 discusses when it is appropriate to use negotiating for Self-leadership. All three chapters contain detailed transcripts of sessions illustrating the process.

This is a technique that some IFS therapists naturally employ when needed. This book should enhance your skill in using this technique successfully in your work with clients.

CHAPTER 1

Updating

Updating is a standard IFS technique. Our clients' protectors are stuck in the past; they believe that our clients are little children who are vulnerable and have few internal or external resources for handling problematic situations. This is, in fact, how we all were as children. Another way to say this is that the protector is protecting a young, vulnerable exile, and it thinks that the client **is** the exile. It doesn't realize that the client has a Self with many more resources than when he or she was a child.

One way to explore this is to have the client ask a protector, "How old do you think I am?" Very often, the protector will mention a childhood age—two or eight, for example. Notice that this is a different question from the one you might ask an exile. You ask the exile, "How old are you?" Of course, you could also ask this question to a protector, and it will often be a young child part, too.

However, when you are preparing a client to do the process of *updating*, have them ask the protector how old it thinks they are.

When to Use Updating

Updating can be useful in the following situations:

The client is asking a protector to step aside and allow the client to work with another protector, but the protector believes that if it steps aside, the other protector will do something destructive that the client can't handle. The client updates the protector about the client's real age, experiences, capacities, and resources so that the protector will feel safe in stepping aside.

The client is asking a protector to give permission for the client to work with an exile, but the protector believes that if it gives permission, something bad will happen to the exile that the client can't handle. The updating reassures the protector that the client can handle it. The protector might also be concerned that if it steps aside, the exile will overwhelm the system with its distress. Updating can be used to reassure the protector that the client can handle an exile's distress.

Updating can also be used in the two common situations in which negotiating for Self-leadership can be used—when you don't have time to heal an exile and after healing an exile when you want to help the protector to let go of its role. These will be discussed in more detail in Chapter 4.

The Updating Process

Here is how a client updates a protector. Once the client has found out how old the protector thinks he or she is, the client tells the protector how old he or she actually is. Then the client shows the protector a series of scenes from the client's life that show the client growing up, maturing, and reaching their current age.

It is also useful to include scenes that show the client accomplishing things, handling difficulties, and generally dealing with a variety of experiences in their lives. This updates the protector as to the client's current capacities.

When clients were young, they were vulnerable and under their parents' power. Our adult clients are no longer dependent children. They are autonomous and in charge of their own lives. Furthermore, in childhood, there wasn't a mature Self present to help, so the protector had to handle this painful state of affairs all on its own. Now that clients are adults, there is a competent, perceptive Self to help in difficult circumstances.

In addition, clients have many strengths and capacities as adults that they didn't have as children. For example, they are more grounded and centered. They may be more assertive, more perceptive about interpersonal situations, better able to support themselves financially, and so on. They have probably accomplished things in their lives and overcome various obstacles. They are adults with much greater ability to handle themselves.

If the protector is blended with the client, **you** can speak directly to the part using direct access and help it see that the client has certain qualities of Self—giving concrete examples of the client demonstrating these qualities with his or her children, friends, or other relationships.

Clients can also show the protector their current life setup and the various people who will support them when needed. They probably have friends, maybe a spouse or lover, perhaps a community they belong to, or a support group they can rely on. They also have your support as their therapist. They have many people they can turn to, if necessary.

Even if clients haven't had much access to Self in the past, it is probably starting to become available because of their IFS therapy with you. However, the protector doesn't realize that the Self is now available to help, so the client needs to make this clear. Since the Self and the protector are now connected, the protector is more likely to listen to the client and trust what they say.

You may ask, "What if a client doesn't have much in the way of adult capacities or resources?" This usually isn't a big problem because clients will certainly have much more ability and support than they did as young children. They will have more capacity simply by being an adult, and they will certainly have more resources than they did as children. After all, the reason that the exile ended up with a burden in childhood is that the client had no one to help handle or process a difficult situation. The client will certainly have more support now than then. If nothing else, the client has you.

If the client doubts their own capacities or resources, this may be coming from a part that needs to be identified and worked with.

If the protector isn't interested in this new information about the client, let the part know that you have some information about the client that might benefit the part at some point in the future, but you can see that it doesn't want that information now. That usually piques the part's curiosity.

The entire updating process is intended to help the protector to understand the client's current age, experiences, capacities, and resources. This information helps the protector to realize that it doesn't need to interfere with the therapy process because of its fear of the client not being able to handle what may happen.

Updating can also be used as part of the process of negotiating for Self-leadership, as will be shown in the next chapters.

CHAPTER 2

Negotiating When the Protector's Fears Are Unrealistic

Let's consider the point in the IFS process when your client has gotten to know a protector and developed a trusting relationship with it. This may make it possible for the protector to cooperate with the client and allow the client (in Self) to take the lead when a situation triggers the protector.

When a situation arises that activates the protector, such as meeting a new person, going out on a date, or interviewing for a job, the protector usually takes over and performs its extreme role. It might cause the client to withdraw, get angry, shut down emotionally, or please people, for example. If it is an Inner Critic Part, it might start pushing and attacking the client.

The protector performs its role because it is afraid of what would happen if it didn't. For example, it is afraid that the client will be judged, shamed, rejected, or betrayed. These fears come from childhood, when the client actually was hurt in one of these ways. However, in the current situation in the client's life, it isn't nearly as likely that the client will be hurt in the way that the protector fears.

In negotiating with a protector, it is best to deal with a specific situation that is coming up soon in the client's life. This allows you to negotiate with respect to the exact parameters of that situation. This chapter deals with the case in which the protector's fears are unrealistic for that situation—in other words, the situation is such that the client won't be hurt in the way it fears. The next chapter shows what to do when there is some validity to the protector's fears in that situation.

The client can learn to negotiate with the protector to allow **Self** to take the lead in this situation so the client can respond in a healthy way rather than in the dysfunctional way that comes from the protector. For example, in a situation in which the client is criticized in a constructive way by her boss, the protector might normally withdraw or get enraged. The client in Self can respond by taking in the criticism, deciding if it seems valid, and then either disagreeing or developing a strategy to improve.

The protector became extreme in childhood because it was dealing with a dangerous or harmful situation—for example, being ridiculed when the client didn't do something perfectly or being yelled at for making a mistake. And the protector became activated because it believes that the same harm is going to happen now in adult life.

Have the client ask the protector what it is afraid will happen in the upcoming life situation. When you know what it is afraid of, let the protector know that you and the client agree that you don't want this harmful event to happen, either. This helps to further build an alliance with the protector before you proceed to negotiate a different response.

Then the client can explain to the protector that the current situation is very different from the childhood one. The client may acknowledge that the protector's role was needed back then and give it appreciation for what it did for the client at that time. Then the client can explain that the current situation is different. The person or people won't hurt the client the way his or her parents did. In addition, the client isn't under their power the way he or she was under the parent's power as a child. Therefore, the protector doesn't need to perform its role.

The client also explains to the protector that because he or she is in Self, the client can make good decisions and handle the situation successfully. The client asks the protector if it would be willing to relax and allow the client (in Self) to handle the situation that is coming up.

Since the client has developed a trusting relationship with the protector, it is likely to listen now. In fact, let me emphasize that it is only possible for this negotiation to work if the client has already created a good connection between Self and the protector so that the protector really trusts that the client understands the protector role and appreciates all its hard work on the client's behalf.

If this hasn't happened, any attempt at negotiation will be perceived by the protector as being misunderstood and dismissed by the client. Consequently, the protector will resist and feel hurt, and may become angry at the client and the therapist. Negotiating for Self-leadership can only work if the protector really trusts the client in Self.

Here's how to tell if this trusting relationship is present. Have the client let the protector know that the client understands what it has been trying to do for him or her. Also, have the client express appreciation for the part's efforts. Then have the client check to see how the part is responding to this. If the part is responding positively, it usually means there is enough trust to proceed. If the part isn't taking in the appreciation, there is more work to do in developing a trusting relationship. (See Chapter 8 in my book *Self-Therapy* for details about how to do this.)

If the protector doesn't agree to relax and let the client handle the situation, the client asks the protector, "What are you afraid would happen if you did relax?" When you find out what the protector is afraid of, have the client explain to the protector why that feared outcome won't happen now. Then ask again if the protector will agree to relax. The protector may then come up with a different outcome it is afraid of. Have the client explain to the protector how that outcome won't happen, either. Then continue the process until the protector has been reassured about all of its fears and is willing to relax.

Keep in mind that parts don't actually want to be performing their dysfunctional roles, even if they won't admit it. In other words, every part has a Self, or a healthy role that it would prefer to perform, but it believes that its extreme role is vitally necessary to prevent serious harm. Therefore, if you can convince a protector that its usual role isn't necessary, it will often be happy to let go of it. The success of this negotiating approach relies on the inherent health of the client's system.

If the protector brings up a fear that might really happen, at least to some extent, you would handle it differently. This situation is covered in the next chapter.

Protector Fears

The following are the common fears that protectors have about what will happen if they don't perform their roles. After each fear, I show how to reassure the protector about that particular fear.

Someone Will Harm or Reject the Client

The protector might be afraid that if it doesn't perform its role, the client will be harmed by someone in the situation. Harm may include judgment, shaming, domination, betrayal, intrusion, anger, physical violence, and exploitation. For example, an angry protector might be afraid that if it doesn't get angry, the client will be dominated by her husband. A different protector might be afraid that the client will be rejected, deprived, abandoned, or not seen by someone in a certain situation. For example, a people-pleasing protector might be afraid that if it doesn't please the client's friends, they will reject her.

Have the client reassure the protector that the people in his or her current life situation are not likely to be harmful or rejecting in the way the client's parents or others were during childhood when the protector took on its role. For example, a client reassures the protector that her husband isn't controlling or that her friends will like her even if she doesn't please them all the time.

If there is a realistic threat, such as the client being harmed or rejected by the people in the situation, deal with it as discussed in Chapter 3.

Sometimes the protector, in its attempt to prevent a certain harmful or rejecting response from people, is actually provoking people to react in the way it fears. This means that, on the one hand, its fear is valid, but on the other hand, if it would let go of its extreme role, its fear wouldn't be valid.

For example, suppose you have an angry protector that gets enraged at people to protect the client from being controlled and judged. Perhaps the client's father was controlling and judgmental, and this protector evolved to protect the client from the father. Now it gets enraged at anyone who reminds it of the father or in situations similar to those that triggered the father. In this case, the protector's reaction is a self-fulfilling prophecy. Its provocative attempts to protect the client are causing the very thing it wants to protect the client from.

Strange as it may sound, this dynamic is not unusual. It is actually quite common for protectors to cause the very outcome they are trying to prevent.

In this case, as part of negotiating for Self-leadership, the client needs to explain this dynamic to the protector. After giving the protector appreciation for protecting the client as a child, he or she spells out how the protector is now causing the very problem it is afraid of by provoking people. The client then explains that if the protector lets go of its provocative role, the reaction it fears from people won't happen.

It isn't usually easy to get a protector to agree to this right away. Even when they understand the consequences of their actions, they are usually still frightened about the client being hurt. After all, they have evidence from the client's adult life that the client does get hurt. The way around this is to ask the protector if it would be willing to give Self-leadership a try as an experiment. This way, the protector can see if the client actually does get hurt when the protector lets go of its role.

Tell the protector that it can jump in with its usual role if people do respond in the way it fears. This will usually work to get the protector to try the experiment, and then it can see that the client is actually not in danger. After that, the protector will be more willing to allow Self-leadership.

The Client Won't Be Able to Handle a Difficult Situation

The protector might be afraid that if it doesn't perform its role, a situation will arise that the client can't handle. For example, a self-effacing protector might be afraid that if it doesn't keep the client small and meek, the client might take public stands on controversial issues and have to deal with disagreement and criticism. The protector expects the client to be devastated because that is what happened when he was a child and was criticized harshly by his parents.

Have the client reassure the protector that the client is a competent adult with many more strengths and capacities than he or she had as a child, so if there are disagreements or criticism, he or she can deal with them. Furthermore, the client has much more in the way of external support now than during childhood. He or she has friends, family, a therapist, and so on, who can help him or her deal with the situation. This is the updating process discussed in the last chapter.

It isn't necessary that clients have a high degree of strength and support—they just need to have more than when they were children and enough to handle the situation. If a client doesn't have the chops to handle the situation that is coming up, negotiating for Self-leadership won't be possible in that situation until he or she does.

A Painful Exile Will Be Triggered

The protector might be afraid that if it doesn't perform its role, something will happen that triggers an exile who is holding pain or trauma, which will be too much for the client. For example, if a protector doesn't withdraw from conflicts as it usually does, it may be afraid that someone will get angry at the client, which will trigger an exile who is terrified of anger.

There are two possibilities:

1. The exile has been largely healed, so this won't happen. Maybe this exile has been triggered in the past, but if it does get triggered now, it's reaction will be mild. In this case, reassure the protector about this.

2. The exile is still in a lot of pain. In this case, reassure the protector that if this exile does get triggered, the client will take some time out to get into Self and take care of the wounded exile. The client may not have been able to do this before therapy, but now the client has the ability to care for a wounded exile. Therefore, the exile won't overwhelm the client, and the client's Self will comfort and nurture the exile.

If the exile hasn't been healed and the client doesn't yet have the capacity to stay in Self and nurture an exile, negotiating for Self-leadership won't be possible until he or she does.

The Client Will Do Something to Bring on Negative Consequences

The protector might be afraid that if it doesn't perform its role, the client will take some action that will be detrimental to the client or will trigger people in the situation to be harmful or rejecting. For example, Joe had a taskmaster protector that was afraid that if it didn't push him to work hard, he would procrastinate about an important project, leading to failure and rebuke.

In this case, the protector is worried about a part that it is polarized with or was polarized with in the past. Have the client reassure the protector that the polarized part has been healed and will no longer take the destructive actions that it did in the past. Or at least make it clear that the polarized part has a good enough relationship with Self that it won't take over and cause problems. For example, Joe can explain that he has worked through his tendency to procrastinate, so his taskmaster can relax and allow Joe's Self to make sure that the project gets done.

If the polarized part hasn't been transformed or at least become connected to Self, negotiating for Self-leadership isn't possible until it has.

The Protector Will Be Banished

The protector might be afraid that if it doesn't perform its role, it won't have a job anymore and will be banished. Have the client explain that if the protector realizes that its role is no longer necessary, it can choose any other role in the client's psyche. It won't be banished.

Negotiating for Self-Leadership with a Perfectionist Protector

Let's look at an example of this negotiating process. Suppose the protector is a Perfectionist Inner Critic, which demands that the client's work be perfect and attacks when it thinks it isn't. The Perfectionist keeps the client from writing, performing, or producing anything, even if no one will see it, because it can't stand to produce anything that isn't flawless, and no one's work is flawless at first.

This Critic tends to become especially activated when the client is learning a skill or experimenting in a creative way with something new. The Perfectionist is afraid to let the client come up with or produce anything because it may not be very good at first, which is frightening for this part. The client was harshly criticized or shamed for not being perfect in the past, and the Perfectionist is trying to prevent this from happening again.

Let's look at how you might help a client negotiate with this type of Perfectionist Critic. There are two possibilities:

1. No one will see what the client will produce. In this case, the client can explain to the Perfectionist that they are safe from criticism. Initially, the client will be producing work that may not be very good, but that is to be expected, and it may even be necessary for learning or experimentation. The client's work is just a rough draft and will be improved or rewritten many times before it gets finalized. Therefore the protector doesn't have to worry about its quality at all. The client won't show his or her work to anyone until it is improved to the point of being very good; therefore, the client will be safe from criticism.

2. The client **will** be showing his or her work to a teacher, a colleague, or someone else. In this case, the client can explain to the Perfectionist that these people know that the work is at an early stage or that the client is just learning or experimenting. These people don't expect the client to be excellent yet. If they do criticize the work, it is only aimed at helping the client learn or improve the project. Therefore, the Perfectionist can relax and allow the client to operate without being concerned about how perfect the output is. Remind the Critic that these people aren't the parents or grade-school teachers (or whoever originally criticized the client).

If one of these people **is** harsh, that would mean that the Perfectionist's fears are somewhat realistic. We will deal with this in Chapter 3.

The client can reassure the Perfectionist Part that it **does** have an important role to play in helping the client to improve the work, but its input must come at the right time, which is after the client has produced something that is far enough along for evaluation to be useful. Then the Perfectionist, like a good coach, can offer feedback on what has been done and help the client to improve it. If the client is writing, this shouldn't happen after each sentence but instead at the end of each draft of the piece. Then its input will be helpful.

If the client is in the early stages of a project, or just learning a skill, or experimenting with something new, a critique probably isn't called for yet. It will be needed later on, when the work is somewhat polished. Most important, by holding off until then, the critique won't get in the way of the client's learning or creativity.

Have the client ask the Perfectionist Part if it would be willing to take the chance to let the client produce work without criticism and see what happens. Ask it to let the client (in Self) be in charge of creating the work, and reassure it that there isn't much danger and that the client can handle anything difficult that does occur. The client will then let the Perfectionist know when is the right time for it to bring in its critical skills in a helpful way. It is more likely to agree to this if the client has already connected with it and if the Perfectionist Part trusts the client.

Example Session with Unrealistic Fears

Following is the transcript of a session I did with Mandy, a participant in one of my ongoing groups in which I was teaching about negotiating for Self-leadership. At the beginning of the session, I helped Mandy get in touch with the part that was causing her presenting problem. I will omit that part and just start where we began to work with that part.

> **Mandy:** I would like to work on the part we have identified that sets up my work schedule so that I don't have enough time for fun.
>
> **Jay:** OK. Focus on that part. Let me know when you're in touch with it.
>
> **M:** Yeah. I am, and I think I spend too much time blended with it.
>
> **J:** Well, let's hear from it. Invite that part to tell you what it's trying to accomplish by setting up your schedule in the way it does.
>
> **M:** The part says, "You know, your employment situation is not up to speed, and all these tasks need to be done in order to increase the chances of a better job. You just don't have time to do all the relaxing and sleeping and fun stuff that you want to do." This part feels urgent about this. It's talking a lot about money and the future. It says, "You don't have all that many years left when you'll be able to work, so you really need to get on this." It's riding me pretty hard.
>
> And there's something else, too. It's not only finances —there's something about emptiness, and like …

being invisible, or being like a child playing alone in a room. The protector wants to avoid that.

J: So I understand the financial worries that this part has. I don't understand the other aspect—about being alone.

M: I think it equates being poor with being alone, invisible, and disconnected from other people. (pause) Somehow, I feel really relaxed right now. There's something about articulating this that feels like a relief.

J: Say more about that. What's the relief?

M: Well, I even yawned a little bit. I'm really relaxing. Identifying this belief as coming from a protector breaks its hold over me. Because when I see that it's a protector's belief, it makes it even more clear to me that it's not all that realistic. I mean, it's accurate to the extent that—yes, there's a recession on, and my income is down. But it's ignoring some important things about life. And seeing that relaxes its hold over me.

She has spontaneously unblended from the part.

J: So to use the terminology that we've been using today, it seems like you're seeing that the protector's fears are not entirely realistic.

I had been teaching them about negotiating for Self-leadership and how to check to see if a protector's fears are realistic.

M: Yes, I think that's right. I had a vague sense of this, but it wasn't enough to break its hold on me.

J: So check and see how you're feeling toward this protector right now.

M: I feel very weary. It's so strident and insistent. It's like it has blinders on. It just won't listen.

J: So it sounds like you're not very open to it right now. You're kind of judging it and wanting it to be different. I think you're probably onto something, but it seems that your attitude toward it is judgmental. Is that right?

M: Yeah.

She isn't in Self with respect to the part. A judgmental part is blended with her.

J: So even though I suspect your judgments are accurate, see if the part that's judging this protector might be willing to step aside, just for the next few minutes, so you can get to know this scheduling protector from a more open place.

M: Oh yes, it's very willing.

J: OK, invite this protector to tell you more about what drives it or what it's afraid of.

M: Well, now I feel a little bit like crying, and I think that's the part. Yes, it's desperate. I mean, it actually grabs my hand and says, "This is really bad! This is a scary situation. We've got to do something about this." This is all it sees.

J: It's desperate.

M: Yeah, it says, "Nothing has panned out with your money in the long term, and that means that I have to keep you going full speed ahead."

J: Ask it what it's afraid would happen if it didn't push so hard. If it left you a little room to have more fun and relaxation, what is it afraid would happen?

M: It's afraid that I would fritter my life away. It's afraid that I would use up the rest of my savings and just go completely bare-assed into my old age. That's it.

J: So it's really worried about your financial future—really you would be headed for disaster if it didn't just push you incessantly.

M: Yes, yes.

J: So even though you don't agree with that and you can see that it's pushing too hard, can you also see that it has your best interests at heart, and it's trying to protect you from something it's really afraid of?

M: Yes, it's very clear to me how very blended I have been with it.

J: For right now, just let the protector know that you appreciate what it's trying to do for you. If you do.

Expressing her appreciation for the part helps to develop a trusting relationship with it, which is essential for negotiating for Self-leadership to work.

M: Oh, yeah. I mean, it's been a complete trouper. It has been very valiant in using every scrap of energy to protect me, for sure.

J: (pause) See how the protector's responding to your appreciation.

M: Well, it's very grateful. I feel like crying right now. I have the sense that it put its head on my shoulder and just sobbed because it's so exhausted. It's been working so hard for so many years.

J: OK, that's good to know. It's really exhausted with this role. Even though it feels like it has to do this job, it's really exhausted.

Once Mandy made a good connection with the protector, it could admit to itself that it is really tired of its role. This is good preparation for it being willing to let her lead.

M: Yeah, it's totally exhausted with it.

J: Let the protector know that you are going to help it not have to push so hard without endangering your finances.

M: Well, I'm telling it, "You've done great, and clearly this way hasn't brought about what you hoped, so let's try another way."

J: You certainly understand that there are legitimate concerns about your finances. You're not doubting that. But you seem to be aware that it would be possible for you to have a schedule that allowed more fun and relaxation without endangering your ability to find a job and make money. Is that right?

I am spelling out why the protector's fears aren't realistic so she can use that information to reassure it.

M: Yes.

J: So just take a moment now and explain that to the protector. Explain what you have in mind and how it's not going to cause the problems that this part's afraid of.

M: So I did tell the protector this, and, by the way, it seems to be male. He can hardly believe it. It's not that he's skeptical, but it seems to be a completely new concept to him. He's battle-weary. He's been a soldier for like decades.

J: See if he'd be willing to take a rest and let you set up your schedule from Self instead of his having to do it.

M: He says, yeah. I mean, he just sat down and slumped over, nodding. He's so tired, and I think he gets the sense now that I have some capacity that he didn't see before. He was so terrified that he didn't see my capacity to discern the right things to do for my financial future. This means I can afford to let go of extraneous work so I don't overwork myself and get sick.

J: So even though we haven't done an official updating, he can see your capacities, is that right?

Updating would be used to show a protector her current capacities, but it seems to understand them without our needing to do that explicitly. This is probably the result of Mandy's making such a good connection with it.

M: Yeah, I have a sense of him seeing my capacities.

Now we are finished. The protector has agreed to let her lead and sees that she has the ability to choose wisely.

J: OK, so thank him for that. Before we stop, I want to suggest that the next time you are involved in setting up your schedule, make sure to be aware of the work we just did, and if necessary, remind that protector that he can relax and let you do it. Reassure him that you won't slip up on doing what is needed for your finances, but you're also going to set aside some time for fun and relaxation. Remind him at the time, so he doesn't just jump in and set up the schedule the way he usually does.

I am suggesting that, at those moments when the protector might be triggered to take over, Mandy remind him that she can handle it safely.

M: OK.

This is an example of negotiating with a protector whose fears aren't valid. The next chapter explains how to handle the situation when they are.

Chapter 3

Negotiating When the Protector's Fears Are Somewhat Valid

Even though the protector fears come from childhood, it is possible that they are somewhat realistic in the present. That is, if the protector lets go of its role in a certain situation in the client's current life, the client might actually be judged, rejected, shamed, yelled at, or whatever else the protector might be afraid of.

The protector's fear is often much greater than is warranted by what would happen in the current situation. After all, that fear is based on the past. However, whenever there is a grain of truth to the fear, you must reckon with it in negotiating with the protector. This doesn't mean that you can't successfully negotiate for Self-leadership; it just means that clients must be prepared to deal with whatever happens, and they must explain to the protector how they plan to do this.

Clients are probably in a much better position to deal with whatever happens than when they were children. Clients usually have much more internal strength for dealing with situations than they did as children. They also have friends and colleagues to turn to now to get help, advice, and support. Clients are more resilient and self-supporting and probably won't fall apart if something hurtful happens. This means that it is likely that a client will be able to handle whatever the protector is afraid of.

If the client **would** be so triggered that he or she would fall apart, negotiating for Self-leadership is not appropriate. Instead, you would need to work with the exile being protected and unburden it first so the client wouldn't be so strongly triggered. Then the protector may be willing to let go.

First, have the client ask the protector what it is afraid would happen if it did relax and let the client handle the situation from Self. When you find out what the protector is afraid of, if there is some truth to its fear, the client should acknowledge this and explain how he or she is planning to handle the feared occurrence if it happens.

Formulating a Plan

For the protector to be willing to relax and allow Self-leadership, the client must formulate a plan for handling the situation in case the protector's fears prove valid—if the client is judged, dismissed, or shamed, for example. These plans might include any or all of the following:

1. Approaching the impending situation in a way that minimizes the chances of being harmed. For example, the client will approach potentially dangerous people in a calm, grounded manner that isn't likely to trigger them.

2. Getting support in the situation. For example, the client will get help from friends or colleagues about how to handle a difficult situation or even bringing other people into the situation who will be on the client's side.

3. Staying away from toxic people or situations. For example, if the client knows that someone is likely to become enraged or shaming, he or she will make a point of avoiding that person unless there is no other choice. Or the client will choose not to engage with someone when they have been drinking or are testy or otherwise likely to react in a harmful way.

4. Not provoking people. The client will make sure not to interact with a potentially hurtful person in an angry or dismissive way that might trigger them to become angry or judgmental.

5. Caring for the exile if it gets triggered. If the person does harm the client in some way, for example, by being angry or rejecting, the client will plan to take some time out soon afterward to access the exile who has been triggered and give it caring and love from Self.

6. Self-assertion. The client will assert him- or herself in the face of harm or rejection. For example, if Sally is ignored, she will practice restating her opinion or reaching out for connection to give herself the best chance of being received. Or if Don is judged, he will say that he thinks his ideas are valid and will ask for a full hearing and discussion about them.

7. Limit setting. The client will explicitly set limits on harmful behavior. For example, if Jill's husband gets angry and hurtful, she will let him know how much this hurts or scares her. Then she will assert that she won't deal with him until he calms down. If necessary, she will leave the room. If he follows her into another room and keeps it up, she will leave the house.

8. Engaging the other person in a dialogue about changing the relationship. If the client is in an ongoing relationship with a hurtful person, he or she will find a time to sit down with the person when they aren't in the middle of a conflict and have a discussion about the person's harmful behavior. The client will explain to the person how he or she is being negatively impacted by the person's behavior. The client will own her feeling reactions but also ask the person to consider attempting to change so the relationship can feel safer to the client.

Of course, many of these plans involve actions that may be difficult for some clients to take. They may need coaching from you and perhaps additional work on parts of them that would interfere with these self-protective strategies. If a client can't manage to create or enact such a plan when it is needed, negotiating for Self-leadership isn't appropriate.

Once the client, with your help, has formulated a plan for dealing with possible problems, the client explains this to the protector and asks if it would be willing to relax and allow the client to take the lead in that situation. Since the client has already made a good connection with the protector and has now addressed its concerns, the protector is likely to agree.

If the protector still isn't ready to relax, there may be something else that the protector is afraid of. Have the client ask the protector what it is afraid of now. Then help the client to formulate a plan for handling that fear, and have the client explain the plan to the protector. Keep going until all the protector's fears have been addressed.

Notice that by formulating such a clear plan that includes

interacting with the world from strength, the client is showing the protector the power and clarity of Self. This will help the protector to trust the Self and agree to allow Self to lead.

In fact, remember that the relationship between the client's Self and the protector is crucial to the negotiation being successful. No amount of logical explanation can substitute for a good internal relationship between Self and a protector.

Negotiating with a Perfectionist Protector with a Realistic Fear

In the last chapter, we talked about how to negotiate with a Perfectionist Part for Self-leadership when it is afraid of having the client's work judged if it doesn't push the client to be perfect. We explored how to do this in the situation in which these fears are unrealistic because the client wouldn't be judged. Let's now look at the other side.

Suppose the people evaluating a client's work **are** harsh and judgmental. Then the client will want to make a serious effort to be sure the project meets their standards so as to minimize the chances of being attacked, but without being perfectionistic about it. However, even if the client does get judged or shamed, he or she can probably handle that. The client isn't likely to fall apart like as in the childhood situation. The client probably has many more internal and external resources for dealing with this situation than in the past.

As mentioned above, if a client **would** indeed get triggered too strongly in the situation, you can't successfully negotiate for Self-leadership. Instead, you will have to work with the client on accessing and unburdening the exile(s) being protected.

In the case in which clients can handle potential judgment or shaming, help them devise a plan for how they will respond if their work receives a harsh response. Here are some options:

1. If the judgments are accurate and not harsh, clients will endeavor to learn from them and not get triggered.

2. If the judgments are accurate but harsh, clients will learn from them and will also say something like the following: "I appreciate your feedback, but I would prefer if you could convey it in a more kindly way."

3. If the judgments are inaccurate, clients will work on asserting themselves in standing up for their point of view while also looking to find common ground with the person judging their work.

4. If necessary, clients will set limits on evaluations that are so harsh or shaming as to cause them emotional harm, whether or not the judgments are accurate. For example, a client might say, "It isn't OK to yell at me like that, whether or not you are right."

Example Session with a Realistic Fear

This is the transcript of a session with Karen, a participant in one of my groups. I was teaching the group about negotiating for Self-leadership.

Karen: I was being trained for a new position in my company, and at some point I was told that I would not get the position. This dismissal was done in a way that was extremely traumatic and hurtful to me. It happened about ten months ago. Since that time, I've been feeling a lot of hurt and grief, and more recently

I realized that I'm feeling a lot of anger.

So it's become obvious to me that I need to speak to my boss and tell him my reaction to the way I was treated. I have a specific body symptom related to holding back my anger about this incident. The part creating this symptom told me very clearly that until I express this anger, it's going to keep on bothering me. So my body is telling me that it is imperative to do this. But I remember other times when I've expressed anger toward my boss, and I've always been cut off and dismissed.

So there's a part of me that's saying, "Hey, let's not express this anger. There will be negative consequences. And that part actually has some real experience to validate that fear.

Jay: OK. We need to work with the protector that says, "Don't express your anger." Tell me, have you worked with this protector before?

K: No, I haven't.

J: OK, we'll start there. Go inside and contact that protector. Do you feel it in your body, or hear it, or see an image of it? Let me know when you're in touch with it.

K: It's showing up as a voice in my head. I hear more the tone of the voice than the actual words. It's like, "da da da da da. It's better not to get angry because..." And I don't know what the rest of the words are. Just, "Quiet it down. Keep it down. Don't get angry. It's not going to work." That's where it is at the moment.

J: Check and see how you're feeling toward that part right now.

K: Part of me is feeling really angry with it, and part of me is actually curious about it, wants to find out more about it.

J: So ask the part of you that's angry with it if that part would be willing to step aside for the rest of this session so you can get to know the Quiet-Down Part from an open place.

In IFS, the client always needs to be in Self before working with a protector, and it is especially important when negotiating for Self-leadership because this will only work if the protector trusts the client. So before going further, I must help Karen unblend from the part that is angry at the protector.

K: The angry part just wants to be heard, and what it's saying is, "God damn it. You're going to stop me from expressing my anger yet again!" It's interesting. This part's angry because somebody wants to stop me from being angry.

The "somebody" is the Quiet-Down Part.

J: Good, I'm glad that part's being heard. See if there's anything else it wants to say.

K: I let it know that I want to get to know this Quiet-Down protector to actually free up my anger. It's grumbling a little bit, but it's willing to step back and let us work with the protector. It says, "Well, it better work!"

J: OK. Thank it for being willing to step back. And check and see how you're feeling toward the Quiet-Down Part now.

K: I feel kind of curious.

J: OK. Invite it to tell you what its concerns are about expressing your anger.

K: I just keep hearing this voice saying, "You know it doesn't really work to get angry." It feels like it's very related to my mother. It kind of echoes my mother.

J: That's **your** understanding of the Quiet-Down Part, which I don't doubt is accurate. But just invite the part to let you know what **its** perspective is.

The idea that it is related to her mother didn't come from the Quiet-Down Part, so I suggest that she really get its perspective. This is not just to make sure that Karen is right. It is also to engage with this protector in order to develop a good relationship with it.

K: It just keeps saying things like, "It doesn't work to get angry. It won't get you what you want. It's better to smooth things over." That's its refrain.

J: Ask the Quiet-Down Part what it's afraid would happen if it let you express your anger.

K: It's just saying it doesn't work. I'm not sure what it's afraid of.

J: Ask it. See if it will tell you.

K: It's very alarmed about the question. I think it's getting a little bit afraid that its power and grip on me might be starting to slip.

J: OK. Ask the Quiet-Down Part what it's afraid would happen if its grip on you slipped.

The Quiet-Down Part is reluctant to tell Karen what its motiva-tion is for fear that it won't be able to protect her anymore.

> **K:** Well, it's showing me a picture of my mother in a state of extreme anxiety and agitation and terror. The picture includes my father, who's angry and yelling. My mother is really terrified of his anger.

> **J:** Ask the part to give you some more information about what it's afraid of.

> **K:** It's showing me that if I get angry, I'm going to get beaten, badly beaten by my father. Now I can actually feel a part of me that's like my mother, that's absolutely terrified of his anger.

> **J:** OK. So there's a lot more we could do with that exile, but for the moment, it sounds like you've got a pretty good understanding of what the Quiet-Down Part is afraid of and why it doesn't want you to express anger. Let it know that you understand now.

> **K:** It's saying, "Yes I **told** you there was a good reason for doing what I'm doing."

> **J:** Good. Check and see if it feels like the Quiet-Down Part is starting to trust you at this point.

> **K:** Not very much.

> **J:** Not very much. Ask it what it doesn't trust about you.

> **K:** It doesn't trust my emotional impulsiveness.

> **J:** I see. So it doesn't trust that you won't slip up and get angry. Is that right?

> **K:** Yeah.

J: See if it trusts that you are actually understanding it and connected to it right now.

K: The Quiet-Down Part seems to be saying that I understand part of it, but there's a sense of it holding itself away from me and not really being willing to be seen completely.

J: So ask it what it's afraid would happen if it let you see it completely.

K: It's afraid it would start to dissolve.

J: It's afraid it would start to dissolve. And then it wouldn't be able to protect you?

K: Right, and then I would just be this helpless child in the face of my father's dangerous anger. Yeah, it's just showing me a picture of how it made me into a very reasonable child who didn't provoke my father—a facade of being reasonable, intelligent, and capable, which actually kept him calmed down.

J: So it sounds like it really did protect you from some serious harm when you were little.

K: I believe so.

J: So let the Quiet-Down Part know your appreciation for what it did for you back then.

Giving a protector this kind of appreciation is the best way to develop trust with it.

K: I appreciate that you gave me a strategy for keeping the family calm. It absolutely wouldn't have worked if I had been an angry child. It would have been a chaotic family instead of a relatively calm one.

J: See how the Quiet-Down Part is responding to you now.

K: It's a lot closer. And it's kind of letting me know that it's been working very hard and it looks somewhat tired of its role. It's actually looking ready to give it up.

J: I bet.

Notice that the Quiet-Down Part has completely shifted. Now that it trusts the Self, it realizes that someone else is there who can help. So it doesn't have to hold so tightly to its role, and it can realize that it is actually tired of its role. This happens frequently.

The normal thing to do next with this session using IFS would be to work with the exile who was so frightened of her father's anger. But since I am doing negotiating for Self-leadership, I go in a different direction.

J: Now ask the Quiet-Down Part what it's actually afraid would happen if it allowed you to speak to your boss about your feelings about being passed over for that position.

K: It says that he would just dismiss me and laugh at me. He would diminish me, devalue me. He wouldn't take me seriously.

J: I'd like you to see if you can assess realistically whether the Quiet-Down Part's fear is likely to happen—that your boss would dismiss you and not take you seriously. See if you can make that assessment from Self.

K: (pause) It really depends on how I speak to him. If I speak with strength and clarity, he'll take me seriously.

But if I approach him with an emotional outpouring, I'm more likely to be dismissed.

J: That makes total sense. So it sounds like you could make a plan to speak to him from strength and clarity.

K: Yeah.

J: Sounds good. Ask the Quiet-Down Part if, under those circumstances, it would be willing to let you speak to your boss about this.

K: It's not sure about that. It isn't convinced that I can come from a place that isn't emotional, especially if I am going to talk to my boss about my feelings.

Even though the Quiet-Down Part has softened, it isn't yet ready to agree until she has a solid plan in place to handle what it is afraid of.

J: OK. That makes sense. What is your plan for doing that?

K: I will prepare beforehand exactly what I am going to say so I am clear. And I'll get into a centered place before approaching him so I don't get choked up. Actually, I've talked to some coworkers about this, and a couple of them have offered to coach me on how to talk with him. So that would also be helpful.

J: Good. Explain this to the Quiet-Down Part and see how it feels now about allowing you to do this.

K: The Quiet-Down Part now looks like it has completely laid down its role. It's so worn out that it's barely conscious. It's just completely deflated. I feel a little bit sorry for it. So it's clearly no longer in that role at all.

In this case, not only has the Quiet-Down Part agreed to allow the Self to lead in this situation, but it seems to have transformed and let go of its role altogether. Of course, Karen will need more time to see if this is really true.

> **J:** You might just ask the Quiet-Down Part if there's some other role it would like to adopt in your psyche. It doesn't have to—it's just an option. It can just rest if it wants to. But if it wants to choose something else, it can.

> **K:** It seems to be just fine about observing what happens without taking any particular role. But I notice that I'm feeling Self quite strongly, and feeling it as strength and clarity and groundedness. It feels like the perfect place from which to speak to my boss.

> **J:** So just take a moment to feel that in your body.

> **K:** I actually feel it very much in my body. I feel a lot of presence in my body and a lot of clarity in my head. I have an intention to say very, very clearly what my experience was. I have a sense of setting boundaries around the way I will and will not allow myself to be treated, even though it's after the fact. That feels like a very good place.

> **J:** OK, check and see if the Quiet-Down Part wants to say anything, or if any other parts do, or if you want to say anything to them, before we stop.

> **K:** Well, the Quiet-Down Part is glad that I've found this place of strength. The little exile really needs some attention at some point. I can see how little and scared

she is. I want to let her know that I see her there, and
I'll come back at some point. That seems to be all.

*It's good that she is aware of the exile work that still needs to be
done. Despite the transformation of the protector, the exile is not
yet unburdened.*

J: OK, good, let's stop there.

This session demonstrates negotiating for Self-leadership
in a situation in which there is some truth to the protector's
fears.

CHAPTER 4

When to Negotiate
for Self-Leadership

There are three common situations in which it is useful to negotiate with a protector for Self-leadership:

1. When there isn't time to heal the exile before a problematic life situation will arise

2. When you have healed the exile, but the protector needs additional help in letting go of its role

3. In real time, at the moment of the life situation

Before Healing the Exile

There are many circumstances in which you don't have time to fully unburden the exile that is being protected before the client wants to get the protector to shift its behavior.

For example, one of my clients had complex trauma and therefore a massive number of intense protectors. It took us months to even begin to have access to any of her exiles and even longer to unburden them. In the meantime, she would occasionally encounter a life situation in which a protector was getting her into trouble.

One protector would engage with angry, dangerous men to try to defuse their rage in group situations, even though she didn't need to. She brought up one of these situations that was coming up during the next week and asked for help. I couldn't just say to her, "Wait until we are able to heal your exiles, and then this protector will let go." She needed help now. So I helped her to learn to negotiate with this protector during the session so it became willing to relax its usual destructive role and stay away from a dangerous man.

Another common situation is when I am doing a session with a client and we are near the end of the hour. The client has gotten to know a protector and created trust with it, and we are now ready to access the exile being protected and heal it. However, there isn't time in that session to go through all the healing steps of witnessing, reparenting, retrieval, and unburdening.

However, the client is facing a troublesome situation in the upcoming week that she wants help with. So I will spend a few minutes helping her to negotiate with the protector to allow the Self to lead in that situation. I plan to come back to the exile in the next session, if possible, to do the healing work with it that would then allow the protector to fully relax.

After Healing the Exile

Normally, after you have unburdened an exile, you then reaccess its protector and ask that part if it is aware of the work that has happened and how the exile is transformed and now feels safe. You then ask the protector if it can now let go of its role, and often it can.

However, sometimes the protector is still not ready to do so. This could be because of another exile it is protecting that hasn't been healed yet or for a variety of other reasons (see Chapter 15 in *Self-Therapy*). Of course, you will want to ferret out the reason the protector is holding on and take care of it so the protector can let go.

In addition to this, you can negotiate with the protector for Self-leadership. In other words, you can negotiate with the protector to see if it would be willing to relax and let go of its role because you explain to it how its role is no longer needed. You have a good chance of being successful at this because one important exile has been healed.

Here is an example of how to negotiate for Self-leadership at the end of a session, after an exile has been healed. In this session, George has been working with a protector, which he calls the Slave Driver, that continually judges him and pushes him to overwork.

So far in the session, he has gotten to know the Slave Driver and received its permission to work with the exile it is protecting, called the Little Boy. He has gone through the healing steps with the Little Boy, which has been unburdened and transformed. We will take up the work at that point.

Jay: Now turn your attention back to the Slave Driver. Let me know when you are in touch with it.

George: OK. I see it there.

J: Check to see if it is aware of the work you have just done with the Little Boy and how he has been transformed.

G: Yes. It has been paying attention the whole time. It's kind of amazed that this has happened.

J: Ask the Slave Driver if it might now be willing to let go of judging you.

G: (pause) Well, it feels somewhat better, but it is still concerned that I won't work hard enough to be successful.

J: Ask the Slave Driver what it is afraid would happen if you didn't work that hard.

G: It is afraid of not getting approval from my boss.

J: Remind the Slave Driver that the Little Boy is feeling fine about himself, so he will be OK even without approval from your boss. So maybe the Slave Driver doesn't need to try so hard to get that approval.

I have him remind the protector that the exile has been healed in the hope that this will help it to let go.

G: It's considering that. (pause) Well, it doesn't feel a desperate need for approval anymore, so I can sense that it is relaxing and doesn't have so much charge around this whole thing.

J: Good.

G: But the Slave Driver still isn't ready to completely give up judging. It is afraid of my being lazy and getting bad performance reviews from my boss.

The Slave Driver has relaxed some, but more is needed for it to fully let go.

Jay: Let me check on something. Have you actually been working adequately on the project at your job? Consider this question from Self, not from the Slave Driver's perspective.

I want to find out whether the Slave Driver's fear of George not working enough is valid or whether it is an outmoded childhood fear, so I check with George in Self to see what the reality is. This is to determine whether or not the Slave Driver's fear is realistic.

> **G:** For the most part, I have been working well. Occasionally I procrastinate. Usually that's because I'm afraid that I won't do a job well enough—when there's a feeling of inadequacy.

> **J:** Is it the Little Boy who feels inadequate?

> **G:** Hmm. That's an interesting question. (pause) Yes. It is that part. That's what throws me off. And then a Procrastinating Part comes in to try to avoid feeling inadequate by not trying at all.

> **J:** So explain to the Slave Driver that you aren't likely to procrastinate now that the Boy is feeling good about himself.

Now that the Little Boy is healed, there isn't the same need for protection from the Slave Driver. My suggestion is aimed at helping it realize that.

> **G:** The Slave Driver is listening and seems to be relaxing some.

> **J:** And if the Slave Driver stops judging you, the Little Boy can continue to feel confident. In fact, explain to the Slave Driver that its judgments have been part of the problem. It has been making the Little Boy feel inadequate.

> **G:** It's really thinking about that. It's shocked to even consider that. (pause)

This goes beyond just helping the protector to see that its role isn't needed. I am hoping that it will see that its role has actually contributed to what it is afraid of. This is not uncommon with protectors, and especially with Inner Critic protectors, such as this one.

> **G:** Well, it's trusting me a lot more now, so it's willing to consider that it should stop judging me. (pause)
>
> But it's still worried about my not working hard enough.
>
> **J:** Explain to it that you agree with its goal of working hard in order to do a good job. Remind it that you have been working well most of the time and that, as an adult, you have good work capacities.

Clearly this helped, but not enough. Since the Slave Driver still has other fears, we must address them, one at a time. Here we explain that George has the capacity to work well when in Self, so it doesn't need to push him.

> **G:** I'm telling it that I can plan my work, pace myself, keep up my motivation, and ask for help when I need it. And I commit myself to working well, so it doesn't need to push me. (pause)
>
> It likes that idea, but it's still worried about getting judged by my boss.
>
> **J:** OK. Remind the Slave Driver that you aren't a child anymore, and you're no longer under your father's power.
>
> **G:** I also told it that my boss is pretty reasonable most of the time, unlike my father.

Here we are helping the Slave Driver to see that George is no longer in the old childhood situation and that the present is much safer.

> **G:** The Slave Driver says it still is afraid of the pain that will result from being judged.

> **J:** OK. You could also explain to the Slave Driver that if your boss does judge you and it hurts the Little Boy, you will take care of the Boy just like you did earlier in the session, so he will end up feeling good about himself.

We are reminding the Slave Driver that George can take care of his exile, if necessary.

> **G:** I'm also telling the Slave Driver that if my boss does get unreasonable, I will talk to him about how he is treating me. I won't just put up with it.

This addresses the possibility that there might be a grain of truth in the Slave Driver's fear and how George will handle the situation if there is.

> **G:** That makes the Slave Driver feel better. It says it's willing to try this approach and see if it works.

> **J:** Great! Thank it for that.

We have finally reassured the Slave Driver sufficiently so that it is willing to experiment with allowing Self to lead.

This is an example of negotiating with a protector that wasn't completely willing to let go of its role even after the exile it was protecting had been healed. It also shows how to respond when the protector has a number of different fears; you must reassure it about each one of them.

In Real Time

It is very helpful for the client to follow up on the negotiating in a session with further awareness and attention when the life situation actually happens. Even though the protector has agreed to let Self lead in that situation, it may forget and take over anyway in the heat of the moment.

Therefore, remind your client to be aware when the life situation comes up and to make sure to check and see if the protector starts to take over. If that happens, the client should remind the protector that it agreed to let Self lead in that situation. Then the client can consciously make an effort to handle the situation from Self and not allow the usual dysfunctional behavior that comes from the protector.

Remember that, at the end of the session with Mandy in Chapter 2, I suggested that she be aware whenever she was setting up her schedule and that she remind the protector not to create a schedule with no time for fun and relaxation.

CHAPTER 5

Conclusion

Even though it is usually best to heal the exile behind a protector before trying to get the protector to change its role, there are circumstances when it is useful to negotiate with the protector to relax its role in a specific life situation that is coming up for your client.

This booklet describes the technique developed by Richard Schwartz for negotiating with a protector to allow the Self to lead in these situations. It explains when this is useful to do, how to perform it successfully, and what is required for the protector to be willing to let go.

Help Sheet

The following is a summary of the steps involved in negotiating for Self-leadership.

1. Create a trusting relationship with the protector.

2. Choose a specific life situation that is coming up for the client.

3. Ask the protector if it would be willing to relax and allow the client to lead from Self in that situation.

4. If the protector isn't willing, ask what it is afraid would happen if it did.

5. Reassure the protector about why each of its fears isn't likely to happen.

6. If there is some validity to one of the protector's fears, formulate a plan for how the client will handle that feared outcome and explain this to the protector.

7. Encourage the client to be aware when the life situation arises and remind the protector to allow the Self to lead.

This is an approach that skilled IFS therapists naturally employ when needed. I hope that this booklet will enhance your facility in making it successful.

APPENDIX A

Glossary

Blending. A situation in which a part has taken over a client's consciousness so that the client feels its feelings, believes its attitudes are true, and acts according to its impulses.

Burden. A painful emotion or negative belief about oneself or the world that a part has taken on as a result of a past harmful situation or relationship, usually from childhood.

Exile. A part that is carrying pain from the past, usually a young child part. It has been pushed into the unconscious and exiled from the client's internal family.

Part. A subpersonality, which has its own feelings, perceptions, beliefs, motivations, and memories.

Polarization. A situation in which two parts are in conflict about how a client should act or feel.

Protector. A part that tries to block off pain that is arising inside or to protect a client from hurtful incidents or distressing relationships in his or her current life. A manager or firefighter.

Reparenting* The step in the IFS process in which the Self gives an exile a corrective emotional experience with respect to a harmful childhood situation. Richard Schwartz sees this as a preliminary part of the retrieval process.

---

* This is a term that I introduced that is not part of the official IFS terminology.

Retrieval. The step in the IFS process in which the Self takes an exile out of a harmful childhood situation and into a place where it can be safe and comfortable.

Self. The core aspect of a person that is his or her true self or spiritual center. The Self is relaxed, open, and accepting of oneself and others. It is curious, compassionate, calm, and interested in connecting with other people and the person's parts.

Self-Leadership. A situation in which a client's parts trust the client, in Self, to make decisions and take action in his or her life.

Unblending. A client separates from a part that is blended with him or her in order to be in Self.

Unburdening. The step in the IFS process in which the Self helps an exile to release its burdens through an internal ritual.

Updating. The client helps a protector to see that the client is a competent adult, not a vulnerable child.

Witnessing. The step in the IFS process in which the Self witnesses the childhood origin of a part's burdens.

IFS Resources

IFS Therapists

If you want to find an IFS therapist to work with, consult the website of the Center for Self Leadership, the official IFS organization, at www.selfleadership.org. It contains a listing of therapists who have completed Level 1 of the IFS professional training and can be searched by geographical location. Some of these therapists offer IFS sessions by telephone.

IFS Professional Training and Consultation

The Center for Self Leadership conducts IFS training programs, which I highly recommend, for therapists and others in the helping professions. There are three levels, which are taken one at a time. Level 1 usually consists of six three-day weekends and is also occasionally offered as a retreat-style training with two week-long sessions. These training programs are held in many cities in the U.S. and in Europe. The leaders are excellent, and the curriculum is well designed. These are experiential trainings, so you learn about IFS by working with your own parts and practicing doing sessions with others in the training. There is an emphasis on building community in the training group, which fosters personal and professional connection. See the CSL website, www. selfleadership.org, for details about training locations and schedules.

I lead IFS consultation groups over the telephone, and I offer a variety of training courses and workshops, many by telephone. See my IFS website www.personal-growth-programs.com for a complete list of offerings.

IFS Courses and Groups

I teach courses for the general public in which people learn to use IFS for self-help and peer counseling. They can be taken by telephone or in person in the San Francisco Bay Area. Each course consists of either six weekly meetings or a weekend workshop. Some of the courses are taught by my wife, Bonnie Weiss, and other highly skilled IFS therapists and teachers. Some of these courses are available as downloadable recordings. We also offer IFS courses and workshops on polarization, procrastination, eating issues, intimacy, communication, and other topics.

I also offer ongoing IFS therapy groups in person as well as ongoing IFS courses over the telephone. See www.personal-growth-programs.com for more information and a schedule of courses and groups.

IFS Books

Introduction to the Internal Family System Model, by Richard Schwartz. A basic introduction to parts and IFS for clients and potential clients.

Internal Family Systems Therapy, by Richard Schwartz. The primary professional book on IFS and a must-read for therapists.

The Mosaic Mind, by Richard Schwartz and Regina Goulding. A professional book on using IFS with trauma, especially sexual abuse.

You Are the One You've Been Waiting For, by Richard Schwartz. A popular book providing an IFS perspective on intimate relationships.

Self-Therapy: A Step-by-Step Guide to Creating Wholeness and Healing Your Inner Child Using IFS, by Jay Earley. Shows how to do IFS sessions on your own or with a partner. Also a manual of the IFS method that can be used by therapists.

Self-Therapy for Your Inner Critic, by Jay Earley and Bonnie Weiss. Shows how to use IFS to work with inner critic parts.

Resolving Inner Conflict, by Jay Earley. A professional booklet that shows how to work through polarization using IFS.

Working with Anger in IFS, by Jay Earley. A professional booklet that shows how to deal with the various ways that anger can arise in an IFS session.

Illustrated Workbook for Self-Therapy for Your Inner Critic, by Bonnie Weiss. A graphic support containing illustrations from the book in large format and grouped for easy understanding.

Parts Work, by Tom Holmes. A short, richly illustrated introduction to IFS for the general public.

Bring Yourself to Love, by Mona Barbera. A book for the general public on using IFS to work through difficulties in love relationships.

IFS Articles and Recordings

The Center for Self Leadership website, www.selfleader ship.org, contains professional articles by Richard Schwartz on IFS. He has produced a number of excellent videos of IFS sessions he has conducted that can be purchased from the website. There are also audio recordings of presentations from past IFS conferences.

Bonnie Weiss and I have downloadable recordings of IFS demonstration sessions to help people learn the IFS process. We also have recordings of our IFS courses for the general public for purchase. See our website www.personal-growth-programs.com for details.

IFS Conferences and Workshops

The annual IFS conference is an excellent opportunity to delve more deeply into the Model and network with other professionals. Richard Schwartz leads week-long personal growth workshops open to the public at various growth centers in the U.S. and Mexico. Other professional work-shops and presentations on IFS by Schwartz and other top IFS trainers are also offered. See www.selfleadership.org for details.

My Websites and Applications

My IFS website, www.personal-growth-programs.com, contains popular and professional articles on IFS and its application to various psychological issues, and more are being added all the time. You can also sign up for the email list to receive future articles and notification of upcoming courses and groups.

My personal website, www.jayearley.com, contains more of my writings and information about my practice, includ-ing my therapy groups.

The Pattern System website, www.patternsystem.com, includes articles, books, courses, and other information.

I have created an Online Community, www.personal-growthconnect.com, where people can connect with others who are doing IFS work, find partners for IFS peer counsel-

ing, share their work with each other, and get their ques-
tions answered.

Made in the USA
San Bernardino, CA
05 March 2014